Jalen Hurts: The Inspiring Story of One of Football's Star Quarterbacks

An Unauthorized Biography

By: Clayton Geoffreys

Table of Contents

Foreword

Jalen Hurts was selected by the Philadelphia Eagles in the second round of the 2020 NFL Draft. He quickly rose to become the Eagles' starting quarterback towards the end of his rookie season and even led the team to their first Super Bowl appearance in six years. The 2022 season earned him spots in the Pro Bowl and as a Second-team All-Pro. Anticipation builds as fans look forward to what Hurts will bring to the team in the coming years following their impressive run to Super Bowl LVII. Thank you for purchasing *Jalen Hurts: The Inspiring Story of One of Football's Star Quarterbacks*. In this unauthorized biography, we will learn Jalen Hurts' incredible life story and impact on the game of football. Hope you enjoy and if you do, please do not forget to leave a review!

Also, check out my website at claytongeoffreys.com to join my exclusive list where I let you know about my latest books. To thank you for your purchase, you can go to my site to download a free copy of *33 Life Lessons: Success Principles, Career Advice & Habits of Successful People*. In the book, you'll learn from some of the greatest thought leaders of different industries on what it takes to become successful and how to live a great life.

Cheers,

Clayton Geoffreys

Visit me at www.claytongeoffreys.com

Introduction

There is no moment more exciting in sports than a game-winning opportunity. The crowd goes crazy, but rarely does anyone ever look to the team that just lost the game. They are merely an afterthought of history.

Very few people remember that the Buffalo Bills have done something that no other team in NFL history has done. They are the only team ever to go to four straight Super Bowls. But nobody really remembers that or even mentions it because they lost all four times they went!

Just getting to the Super Bowl is one of the greatest team accomplishments any franchise can achieve, but people only look to the winners. Fans don't want to deal with the heartbreak. We only want the celebrations.

Few players in the history of sports have suffered a worse heartbreak in front of millions of people than former Alabama quarterback Jalen Hurts. He led the

Tide to the national championship game—only to be released at halftime.

His replacement, Tua Tagovailoa, would go on to lead Alabama to that championship and replace Hurts as the starting quarterback in the following season.

So, how do you come back from that kind of public humiliation? It took someone of great character, resolve, and integrity to pick himself back up and return to the football field. Jalen Hurts is all that and more.

Hurts was born and raised in Channelview, Texas, just outside of Houston. His father is a high school football coach there, and his mother is an elementary school teacher.

Hurts grew up around the game of football. When he was old enough, his father took him to practices and games. Hurts acted as the team's water boy for as long as he could remember. Hurts picked up the game from his father and his older brother, who also played quarterback for their father.

When it came time for Hurts to take over at quarterback, his father brought him along slowly. During his junior year, Hurts helped his father get his first winning season as a coach.

Hurts also played basketball and baseball in high school, but decided to give them up. He realized that playing those sports would not help him become a better football player. Instead, he became a champion powerlifter, which would help his leg strength and turn him into the great runner that he would later become.

During his senior year, Jalen Hurts was a four-star recruit. He led Channelview to the state playoffs and another winning season. After the season, Hurts made the decision to play for Alabama and head coach Nick Saban.

Hurts enrolled at Alabama in January, and by the second game of the season, he became the first true freshman to ever start at Alabama for Saban. He would lead the Tide to a 12-0 regular season record. In the postseason, they would win the SEC Championship and the first round of the College Football Playoffs. Finally, in the championship game, Alabama lost to Clemson. It was the first loss of Hurts' college career.

During Jalen's sophomore season, Tua Tagovailoa arrived on campus. Hurts won the starting job and led Alabama to an 11-1 record and another trip to the College Football Playoffs. But, in the championship game, Hurts would be replaced by Tagovailoa and could only watch as someone else won his national championship.

After the game, Hurts thought about transferring, but he did not want to sit out an entire season. Instead, he remained at Alabama for his junior season, playing sparingly. In the SEC Championship game, though, he got his shot. Tagovailoa went down with an ankle injury. Hurts came in and promptly led Alabama to a thrilling come-from-behind win. It was sweet redemption for Hurts.

Ultimately, Hurts transferred to Oklahoma to work on his passing skills with head coach Lincoln Riley. Jalen led the Sooners to an 11-1 regular season record as their undisputed starting quarterback, and eventually a Big 12 title. He would come in second place for the Heisman Trophy behind LSU's Joe Burrow. Oklahoma would lose in the opening round of the College Football Playoffs to Burrow and LSU, but nevertheless, his time at Oklahoma was redemption, and confirmation that he was ready for the NFL.

Thus, Jalen Hurts entered the NFL draft. But despite being one of the most productive college quarterbacks ever, scouts still had their doubts about him. Hurts slipped all the way to the second round, and into the grasp of the Philadelphia Eagles.

When Hurts got to Philly, there was already a starting quarterback. Four years earlier, the Eagles had spent a first-round draft pick on Carson Wentz. Wentz began his NFL career as an emerging star in the league, but then began to struggle. When Hurts arrived, Wentz would start the team's first 12 games—but he led the league in sacks, interceptions, and turnovers. Hurts was named the team's starter for the final four games of the season, going 1-3.

During his second season, Hurts was able to lead the Eagles to the playoffs, but they eventually lost to the Tampa Bay Buccaneers and the legendary Tom Brady. That experience propelled Hurts into the next season.

In his third season, Hurts led the Eagles to a team-record 14 regular season wins. The Eagles blew out the Giants and 49ers in the playoffs and made it all the way to the Super Bowl.

In the Super Bowl, Hurts had one of the best games in history. He tied a record by rushing for three touchdowns in the game. But sadly, the Eagles still lost to Patrick Mahomes and the Kansas City Chiefs.

Nevertheless, Jalen Hurts has turned himself into one of the best quarterbacks in the NFL after suffering through that adversity while in college. He has risen to helm one of the most formidable teams in the league, and proven himself to be one of the league's most unstoppable quarterbacks. This is how he did it.

Chapter 1: Childhood & High School

The Coach's Kid

There is something to the idea that a coach's kid makes a better football player. From the time they are born, they watch as their father dedicates himself to the game and devotes himself to teaching his son everything he knows. The coach's kid grows up around the game, undoubtedly knowing the ins and outs of football better than their peers. They also get to see just how much work goes into the preparation for every game.

Nearly every coach brings their family into the game with them if they get the opportunity. It is often the only way that they can get a chance to see their children during the season! In fact, many coaches' kids will show up at practices and games to be the ballboy or the waterboy for the team. It is almost instinctual that those kids will pick up the game through that exposure and follow in their father's footsteps.

Philip Rivers' father Steve was one of the best coaches in the history of Alabama high school football. Indeed, he was selected to the Alabama High School Hall of Fame. So, when Phillip went to North Carolina State, it came as no surprise that Steve followed his son to the Tar Heel State and took over another coaching program there.

After his Hall of Fame career in the NFL, Philip Rivers followed his father into coaching, and he is now a varsity football coach in Florida. One day, Philip will no doubt be coaching his own children in high school.

There are a number of coaches who bring their children with them to games and practices, and many of those kids eventually become coaches themselves. Patriots Head Coach Bill Belichick brought his son Steve with him to games and practices early in his career with the team. And now, Steve has become a coach with the Patriots.

This was also the way that Bill Belichick learned the game as well. His own father Steve (his son's namesake), was a coach and scout at the Naval Academy for more than 30 years. After graduating from Wesleyan University in Connecticut, Bill went down to the Naval Academy and became an assistant coach with his father. (As an interesting side note, one of the other coaches on that staff was a young Nick Saban.)

But there are thousands of high school football coaches across the country who work hard every day for their players, come home tired, and try to teach their own children the game.

Averion Hurts Sr. is one of those coaches. Averion was a high school football star himself at Channelview High School in Texas. He received a scholarship to play football and run track at Howard Payne University in Brownwood, Texas. He was an all-conference football player and a six-time All-

American in track and field as well. He would eventually graduate with a degree in marketing.

After spending four years in the corporate world, Averion moved into education. After two more years toiling in the classroom, he went back to the football field to become a coach. While working as a coach for Douglas MacArthur High School in San Antonio, Texas, he met and fell in love with Pamela. The two would be married in the early 1990s.

In 1993, their first child, Averion Hurts Jr., was born. After working his way through the assistant ranks in Texas, Averion Sr. ended up going back to his alma mater and ultimately became the head football coach at Channelview High School.

On August 7, 1998, Pamela and Averion welcomed their second son, whom they named Jalen. When Jalen was eight, the family moved to Channelview for Averion's new job. By then, Jalen had practically been born on the football field. By the time he was born, his father had already been a football coach for four seasons. And Jalen would spend as much time as he could with his father on the sidelines.

"I have a foundation kind of set for myself, but my parents kind of did that for me," Jalen said of his parents. "And I think being a coach's kid, they created habits for me to see things a certain way, have the wisdom that I have, and I give all the credit to them. He's (Averion) the reason I am who I am on the field, off the field. Being a coach's kid, I talk about it all the time, but I truly lean on that. To always compete, to always give my best, to always show respect to the people around me, I think those are some core things that he instilled in me. I always go back to my experience and my time of being a coach's kid. Those are times I wish I could go be that kid again and do that again. Those are special times. But I learned so much, and I saw him lead."[i]

But it was not just his father that had an influence over Jalen. His mother, who was an elementary school special education teacher, made sure that he stayed grounded. No matter what was happening on the field, Jalen always finished his schoolwork first.

But despite his deep family ties to football, *baseball* was actually Jalen's first love. Like all kids, he would decorate his room with posters of his favorite players. When Jalen landed on the cover of *Sports Illustrated* in 2023, he told the magazine that he would put athletes on his wall, but his favorite was Bryce Harper of the Washington Nationals.

"Being on the cover of SI goes back to my childhood," Jalen said. "I put a couple of different professional athletes on my wall as a kid, and I have a very meaningful wall back home in my room and I tell my mom never to take it down because I know it'll be beautiful in the end, when it's all said and done. Bryce Harper, who's a guy in this city. When I had baseball dreams, you know, he was a guy that I always followed and had a lot of respect for. Seeing all the athletes on the cover, a lot of athletes that I watched for my whole entire life, that I've looked up to, and had a lot of admiration for. To be that figure for the next generation, coming into this time, this season, it's an exciting thing."[ii]

Harper made the cover of *Sports Illustrated* himself in 2009 as a 16-year-old. He was touted as "Baseball's Chosen One." After starting his career in Washington, he signed a free-agent contract with the Philadelphia Phillies. Years after having Harper's photo on his bedroom wall, Jalen and Harper would become the faces of their respective teams in Philly—and good friends. The two routinely keep in contact and play in charity softball events together on the rare occasions that their offseasons overlap.

Jalen demonstrated a natural athleticism from an early age that could have easily translated to a number of different sports. He also played basketball through his middle school years, but one day, he told his father that he was quitting both baseball and basketball.

At first, Averion did not understand his son's decision to quit two sports that he loved, but then Jalen explained it to him. Jalen said that neither of those sports was going to help him become a better football player.

After he gave up the other sports, Jalen immersed himself in all things football. He was the water boy for his older brother's team and fell in love with some of the players on the team and tried to emulate them.

Jalen mentioned Jackie Hinton, DJ McNorton, and his older brother, Averion Jr., as the players who influenced him the most. All three taped their ankles before games, and so Jalen started doing the same thing before his youth league games.

"I wouldn't be where I am without those guys, those experiences, and those are my number one supporters back home," Jalen said. "For me to be on the stage I'm on, have the opportunities that I have, and have done the things I've done, I know it means the world to them, too. So, I just want to make them proud."[iii]

All three of those players would go on to play college football and even get into coaching later in life. Hinton played at the University of Houston, McNorton at North Dakota State University, and Averion Jr. played quarterback at Texas Southern and now, like his father, is a high school football coach in Texas.

The one other way that those three helped to influence young Jalen was in the weight room. They taught him the proper way to lift weights, and after Jalen quit basketball and baseball, he would spend his winter and spring in the weight room. That would ultimately become his second sport in high school as he became a champion powerlifter.

Now that Jalen had decided to focus all of his attention on football, he needed to head to high school, where everything that he had learned thus far would be tested and expanded upon. But, unlike other players, Jalen would have to go home with the head coach, so if he made a mistake, he would hear about it all the way home!

Channelview High School

Texas High School football is no joke. The state produces more than 250 FBS players every single year. It has produced some of the best players in the history of the NFL, including Patrick Mahomes, Drew Brees, Earl Campbell, Von Miller, and Adrian Peterson. If iron sharpens iron, then Texas high school football players come out ready to play at the next level after having spent an entire football career against some of the best competition in the country.

Averion Hurts knew that he had something special in his son, Jalen. But at the same time, as a freshman, he knew that his son still had a lot to learn. Having been a high school coach for nearly 20 years by the time his second child entered high school, Averion also knew that if he put 14-year-old Jalen on the field against nearly grown men, he could get hurt.

He wanted to make sure that his son was ready to take over as the starting quarterback, so Jalen began his high school career primarily on the bench. It was an unusual move for a father, but a typical and even smart decision for a head football coach. Channelview started the season 1-1 after a Week 2 victory over Humble High School. But then, the team finished the year on a seven-game losing streak to finish the year at 1-8.

Jalen played only sparingly at the end of some games. Averion made sure to get him varsity action so that he could adjust to the speed of the game. But despite the losing season and the team's clear need, Averion did not rush Jalen into the starting role. Instead, he wanted his son to learn the game, and more importantly, he wanted him to learn humility and service to the entire football community.

The former head coach of Beaumont's West Brook High School, Kevin Flanigan, recalled the moment when he first saw Jalen and realized that there was something special about him.

"It was a subvarsity game on a nasty, damp Thursday night," Flanigan said. "I look over, and there's Jalen standing on our sideline working with the chain crew. You could look at him and just tell he was thinking, 'Okay, this is my role tonight.' It's a great example that he saw himself as *part* of the team, not *the* team. It wasn't like him to say, 'I'm too good for this.' That has always made an impact on me. There's no way he had any idea that I would notice that, and that I would tell that story over the years to illustrate his character. I've told our teams that's how you do it. And that's the number one memory I have of Jalen Hurts—how he conducts himself."[iv]

After a season of learning, Jalen finally took over the starting job as a sophomore. Channelview started out the season 4-0 but then lost their next five games to finish at 4-5. For his part, Jalen was named second team All-District.

After the season ended, Jalen headed back to the weight room and started working out. In Texas, competitive weightlifting is a varsity sport. During his first meet of the season, Jalen was able to squat 385 pounds easily. During the second meet, he put up more than 400 pounds.

At that point, Averion thought he should stop adding weight, but Jalen decided to move up to 440.

"So, I'm thinking 'Okay,'" Averion said. "I didn't say anything. I was waiting because if he were to not get it, I was going to get after him."[v]

Not only did he do 440 pounds, but just a few weeks later, Jalen squatted 500 pounds. That year, Jalen would place third in the Texas state powerlifting meet in the 185-pound category. During his junior season, Jalen would squat 570 pounds, bench press 275 pounds, and deadlift 585 pounds to place second in the state.

"It's tough to get kids to commit, especially quarterbacks, to that level of lifting like he did," Flanigan said. "But again, that's the difference in being good and being great. He just did everything right."[iv]

Once powerlifting season was over, Jalen took up track and field. And he truly took part in both the track and the field. During one particular meet, the entire field had to stop and wait while Jalen finished up throwing the shot put so that he could compete in the 4X100 relay.

Back on the football field for his junior season, some people started comparing Jalen to former Texas A&M star Johnny Manziel. Manziel would win the Heisman Trophy as a freshman for the Aggies, but he would ultimately flame out in the NFL with the Cleveland Browns.

Both Manziel and Jalen were around the same height and played the game in a similar way. They both used their legs to buy time in the pocket and run when necessary, but Averion believed that comparisons were unwarranted.

"Manziel's kind of like a gunslinger to me," Averion said. "Jalen's not a gunslinger. He's just a kid that's really athletic and has the ability to make plays with his legs, but he's a pass-first kid. And for me as a coach, Johnny didn't pick up the playbook. Johnny had one or two reads, and that hurt him in the NFL. Jalen is more of a bigger Russell Wilson type."[v]

No matter the comparison, Jalen was ready for his junior season of football. In their opening night win over Dayton, Channelview scored 69 points, and Hurts dominated the game.

"The moment that stands out to me was the first game his junior year when I realized that he really had matured as a player and that he was different," Averion Sr. said. "We beat some really good teams, and it got to a point where I felt like we walked into the game with the best player on the field. I'd never been in that situation before."[iv]

In the first five games of the season, Channelview was 5-0 and the offense was averaging an astounding 60 points a game.

"The power of his running was something I don't know that he got enough credit for early on," North Shore High School head coach Jon Kay said. "He runs like frickin' Larry Csonka, though he looks light on his feet. People throw around the term 'dual-threat quarterback,' and to me, he's really one of the few that I saw. I just remember truly not knowing how to defend a guy that could run with power, could run with speed, and had such touch and accuracy throwing the ball. He runs so effortlessly that you fall into the trap of thinking he's not that fast. But you don't see anybody catch him."[iv]

But it wasn't just his running ability that helped lead the offense. Jalen was having a great season with his arms as well. During his junior year, he threw for 1,958 yards and 16 touchdowns. He added another 750 rushing yards and 17 touchdowns.

With five wins to start the season, Jalen earned his father his first career winning season as a head coach. But Channelview struggled to end the season, losing four of their final six games and missing out on the playoffs.

Once the season ended, the college coaches started coming around. At first, it looked like Jalen might stay in Texas, with Texas A&M being one of the first schools to offer him a scholarship. But then Alabama and Mississippi State, as well as several other SEC and

Big 12 schools, offered him a scholarship. By the end of his junior season, Jalen was a four-star recruit.

In the spring of his junior season, Jalen and his father took a trip to Alabama and met with coach Nick Saban and his staff. They then took trips to Texas A&M and Mississippi State.

During the summer before his senior season, Jalen was invited to compete in the Elite 11 quarterback competition. The Elite 11 is a yearly quarterback competition that tries to find the best 11 high school quarterbacks in the country. Jalen made it to the semifinals but was not selected as one of the Elite 11 quarterbacks for 2015. Nevertheless, Jalen would be the only player at the camp to become a Pro Bowler in the NFL!

While at the camp, Jalen announced his college decision. He decided that he was going to play at the University of Alabama and for Coach Saban.

"At Alabama, I loved Coach (Nick) Saban's plans for his players," Jalen said. "Not only do they have a great competitive football program, but academically they also do a great job. Their focus is to give you the tools to become a successful man in life, and that is my main goal. I absolutely love what Alabama has in store for their students and athletes. They have lots of history and everlasting tradition. I feel this was the best decision for me, as I am a boy trying to become a man. I am very comfortable with my decision and very blessed to be in this situation. I will be ready to compete at U of A when that time comes. But for now, all I can say is Roll Tide."[vi]

But Alabama offensive coordinator Lane Kiffin was starting to get nervous, even after Jalen made his commitment. Kiffin was nervous because Jalen had not put it out on social media that he had committed to Alabama.

"I think it was Lane Kiffin that asked him, 'Are we good? Are you still committed?'" Flanigan said. "They'd seen nothing on Twitter. Jalen didn't do that stuff. He gave his word. That was enough. Someone at Alabama told him, 'We'd kind of like for you to put it out there, so people know.' People talk about putting the team first and that sort of thing. But very few do it. Very few put the team before themselves."[iv]

What the coaches at Alabama did not understand was that Jalen wanted to keep the focus on his team and not on his personal accomplishments. He also simply did not use social media much, a rarity among athletes of his generation.

To start his senior season, Jalen and Channelview again went 5-0. This time, they averaged 60 points a game, including scoring 82 points in Week 2.

"We thought he had a cannon of an arm," Vidor High School head coach Jeff Mathews said. His team was able to hold Jalen to only 49 points. "We didn't know how surgical he could be. He'd have a small window to get the ball in there, and he wasn't scared to throw it. His senior season, my son Mason is one of our cornerbacks. On the first play, Mason crowded the wide receiver, and Jalen and the receiver just looked at each other. Just like that, a seventy-five-yard touchdown pass … eight seconds into the game. I remember getting on our kids the next morning. I feel bad about that because last week I saw some of the same things happen to the [San Francisco] 49ers."[iv]

Teams tried everything they could to stop Jalen. They even tried doing nothing. Defenses would stand at the line of scrimmage and let him throw the ball. They felt that strategy was better than getting run over!

"Our defensive coordinator, Eric Peevey, was so funny—I've never seen it done before or after," Flanigan said. "He told our defensive players, 'If you get in the backfield, and Jalen's back there, I don't care if you think you can make a play on him or not, do not flush him out of the pocket.' There were several times our D linemen got back there and just stopped. They just froze and tried to hold him in there. If you forced him to throw it, there's a chance someone would drop the ball. But if he took off and ran, it was over."[iv]

But just like in his junior season, once the competition got tougher, Channelview started to fade. They would drop two straight games, but then win two straight. Still, Channelview would qualify for the Texas State Playoffs for the first time in Averion's career. However, they would lose that game 71-21 to Manvel.

Jalen ended his senior season with 1,536 passing yards and 18 touchdowns. He added 941 rushing yards and another 18 touchdowns. He was named the District MVP.

With his high school career over, no one was prouder of Jalen than his father.

"It's truly humbling," Averion said. "And the most important thing to me is watching a young man make goals for himself—you know, things that he wanted, not that I wanted for him—and watch him work so hard and diligently to achieve them. His journey prepared him for now. We've always felt that God had a plan for him, and God had his hands on it. It made him a stronger man on earth. It's humbling as a coach to have such kind words spoken about a former player. When that's your son, it really, really means a lot—the respect guys have for him."[iv]

For opposing high school coaches who had to come up with a plan to stop him, it was a relief to see Jalen head off to Alabama. He would now be taking his skills to the SEC, and *those* coaches would have to figure out a way to stop him.

Chapter 2: College Career

Alabama - Freshman Year

When Jalen Hurts arrived on campus in the winter of 2016, the Alabama Crimson Tide were riding high. They had just defeated Clemson for the national championship, and running back Derrick Henry won the Heisman Trophy. But all that was in the past. Henry was on his way to the NFL, and starting quarterback Jake Coker had also graduated. That left an opening at quarterback, but Hurts was at a disadvantage. During his tenure as the head coach at Alabama, Nick Saban had never started a true freshman at quarterback. Hurts was hoping to be the first.

Arriving in the winter of 2016 rather than the fall of 2017 gave Hurts an advantage over the other freshmen. He would be able to enroll in school early and start working out with the team immediately. It also gave him the opportunity to play in the Alabama spring game and compete for the starting job immediately.

Hurts was competing against Cooper Bateman and Blake Barnett for the starting job. But in his first practice, Hurts made an impression on the entire team. His job was to mimic the starting quarterback for another team. The best defense in the country struggled against the freshman.

"During that practice, he made a couple of plays and a couple of moves, and I knew that he's going to be fine," Averion Hurts said. "He was trying to give them a good picture. But like I told him, that was a situation where you've got the opportunity to let them know now that you can play. My opinion is that during that first week there he showed the coaches that they made the right choice and showed the players that he can play."[v]

In the spring game, Hurts would throw the game-winning touchdown in the game; it was also the *only* touchdown in the game, as the defense dominated. Hurts finished the game with 120 yards passing, but he was sacked five times. In total, Alabama quarterbacks were sacked 11 times.

"I think both guys (Barnett and Hurts) made some good throws," Saban said after the spring game. "Both guys showed their athleticism in terms of ability to extend plays. But there's also many occasions where they should have thrown the ball hot, didn't, got sacked or should have gotten rid of the ball, ran around, lost 20 yards on a sack. So, some of the inexperience shows in some of the negative plays that sort of are like unforced errors in tennis. You don't need to be taking these plays if you really know what you were doing. It has nothing to do with ability. It has everything to do with awareness, experience, knowledge and then reacting to what happens. I think that's going to be the key to the drill with those guys in terms of their development."[v]

Ultimately, Saban decided to go with Barnett as the starter for Week 1 against USC, but Hurts would be waiting in the wings if anything went wrong—and things started to go wrong right from the start. The Tide offense was sluggish in the first quarter, as USC took a 3-0 lead. Midway through the second quarter, Saban turned to Hurts. He immediately showed his skills, hitting ArDarius Stewart on a 39-yard touchdown pass.

With Hurts leading the way, the Tide surged forward to take a 17-3 lead into the half. Then, in the third quarter, Hurts continued to dominate. He hit Stewart again on a 71-yard touchdown to start the quarter. He then ran for two touchdowns to put the game out of reach. Barnett would come back into the game in the fourth quarter merely for mop-up duty in the Tide's spectacular 52-6 win.

After the blowout opening week win, Saban named Hurts the starting quarterback for the Tide. He would be the first true freshman to start for Saban, and the first to start for Alabama since 1984. After the news broke, Barnett announced that he was transferring. He would ultimately leave Alabama later that September and transfer to Arizona State University.

The starting job was now Hurts's. He started his first game in front of the home crowd by throwing two more touchdowns in a win over Western Kentucky.

"We're pleased with the progress that he's made," Saban said of Hurts after the game. "We have a lot of faith, trust, and confidence in him."[vii]

In his second career start, and first against an SEC opponent, it initially appeared that the Hurts magic was about to end. Alabama found itself down 24-3 against Ole Miss in the second quarter. But the Tide were able to close the gap by scoring 14 points in the final 2:30 in the first half, getting within 7. And Hurts wasn't done.

Hurts used both his arm and his legs to orchestrate a brilliant comeback. He rushed for a career-high 146 yards and passed for another 158. Alabama scored two defensive touchdowns in the second half and ultimately won the game 48-43.

The No. 1 Tide next blew out Kent State and Kentucky on their way to a 5-0 start. But that was when the schedule started to get tougher. Alabama had four straight games against ranked SEC opponents right in the middle of their schedule.

First up was No. 16 Arkansas. Hurts took the game over in the first quarter, rushing for two touchdowns. He then threw for another two touchdowns in the blowout 49-30 win. It was his second career four-touchdown game in just six games.

"It works well for us, it's when we play the best," coach Nick Saban said of the offense. "Our quarterback is well-suited for it, and I think we've done a good job as a staff developing the system where it's maybe a little more efficient than when we started doing it a couple years ago."[viii]

Next up was a trip to No. 9, Tennessee. Hurts threw his only touchdown pass of the game in the first quarter, but Alabama only had a 14-7 lead after Alvin Kamara scored for the Volunteers. That was when Hurts took over running.

Hurts rushed for a 45-yard touchdown to end the half. In the third quarter, he rushed for two more touchdowns to give him three on the day. It was his first career three-touchdown rushing game. He ended the game with 132 yards rushing and 172 passing yards. He also added a tackle for a loss. Alabama blew out Tennessee 49-10.

"This is as proud of our team as I've been all year long in terms of playing a complete game against a very good team, especially in a tough environment," Saban said.[ix]

Next up was No. 6 Texas A&M. Both teams entered the game undefeated. The Tide were up 13-7 at the half, thanks to a Hurts touchdown pass. But early in the third quarter, Texas A&M took a 14-13 lead.

Alabama would end the game with a statement 21-0 run. Hurts hit Calvin Ridley to retake the lead, and after a defensive touchdown, Hurts scored the final touchdown on a 37-yard run. Alabama would hold on to win 34-14.

The final game in Alabama's daunting four-game gauntlet against ranked teams was a trip to LSU. For three quarters, the two defenses dominated the game. Neither team was able to do much on offense, and heading into the fourth quarter, the game was tied at zero.

Early in the fourth quarter, Hurts was finally able to escape the grasp of the LSU defense, and he slipped into the end zone for the game's only score. The Tide would add a field goal to win 10-0.

"He has great poise. I don't think the stage is too big for him at all," Saban said about Hurts. "He expects a lot of himself and we expect a lot of him because he's in a role that has tremendous responsibility. He has handled that very, very well. You can talk about winning ugly and maybe it wasn't always pretty, because we certainly didn't execute and do things the way we'd like, but you've got to give LSU a lot of credit. It was a tough atmosphere for us out there. But our defense was outstanding. We've got some pretty hateful guys that play defense around here that are pretty good competitors. When they get challenged a little bit, they usually respond and I think they responded really well tonight."[x]

Alabama was now 9-0 and had just won four straight games against ranked teams. Hurts celebrated by throwing for a career-high 347 yards and 4 touchdowns in a blowout win over Mississippi State, and then another three touchdowns in a win over Chattanooga.

The top-ranked Tide were 11-0 heading into the Iron Bowl against Auburn, and freshman quarterback Jalen Hurts was riding high.

"I truly believe he's built to handle this," his father, Averion Hurts, said. "Like I tell him, if he stays focused and stays true to his values, he'll be fine. In life, you see people make bad choices, and he's intelligent enough to be able to look at people make bad choices and realize that that's not a choice that he wants to make. He's not a party animal. He's a quarterback. He's a good-looking kid. He can talk. He could go out and do whatever he wants and have all the fun he wants. But he also knows that sometimes all that stuff comes with trouble, and he has enough role models that have told him that. So, he'll go out sometimes, but he doesn't like a lot of attention. That's why he's not really on social media."[v]

In his first-ever Iron Bowl, Hurts started the game by throwing his first pass to Auburn. The Alabama defense helped him out by holding the Tigers to a field goal. But on the next possession, Hurts threw another interception. Again, the Tide defense bailed him out, forcing Auburn to punt.

If it were any other quarterback, two straight interceptions would have ruined his day, but not Hurts. He ended the quarter by hitting Damien Harris for a 17-yard touchdown to give Alabama a 10-3 lead.

After the teams spent the second quarter exchanging field goals, Hurts opened the scoring in the third quarter with a four-yard touchdown run to put the game away. He would add a second touchdown pass for good measure as Alabama rolled 30-12.

That hard-fought win earned the Tide a trip to Atlanta to play for the SEC Championship against Florida. The Gators opened the game with a touchdown against the Alabama defense. But that would be it for Florida. Statistically, Hurts had one of his worst games of the season, but that was only because he did not have to spend much time on the field.

Alabama's defense returned an interception for a touchdown in the first quarter, and the special teams followed that up with a blocked punt to take over the game. After that, the rout was on. Hurts did throw a touchdown pass in the second quarter, but he sat out most of the fourth quarter. Alabama went on to win the SEC Championship 54-16.

"First of all, so very proud of our team for, first of all, having an undefeated season, but secondly, for winning the SEC Championship," Saban said after the game. "I think to do that three years in a row is a really significant accomplishment, especially these guys who have been challenged all year long by playoff game after playoff game, but this was the first championship game we had, and they certainly responded well in the game, and I'm very proud of them. I'm happy for our fans. I'm happy for our university. I'm happy for

Reuben for being the MVP of the game. The 25th anniversary of this game, I think this is a great competitive venue we started 25 years ago. Coach Stallings and Coach Spurrier were here today and great to see them back. This is something I've participated in a few times, and other than a national championship game, there's nothing better. Just can't tell you how proud I am of our players."[xi]

Alabama was now the top seed in the College Football Playoff. They headed back to Atlanta to play in the Peach Bowl against Washington. The Huskies shocked the Tide when they scored the game's first touchdown halfway through the first quarter. But then Tide running back Bo Scarbrough took over. He rushed for two touchdowns, and the Alabama defense completely shut down the Huskies in a 24-7 win. For Hurts, it was his worst game as a college player. He only threw for 57 yards on seven completions. He added another 50 yards rushing. But his stats didn't matter. It was still a win, and the Tide were on their way to the College

Football Playoff Championship Game against Clemson.

The year before, the Tide had knocked off the Tigers 45-40 to win their fourth national championship in seven seasons. But the Tide had not seen an opponent like the Tigers all year. There were no two teams more evenly matched in college football at that time.

Scarbrough picked up where he left off in the semifinals by scoring two touchdowns in the first two quarters of the game. Clemson's quarterback Deshaun Watson brought the Tigers to within seven before the half.

The Tide added a field goal early in the third quarter, but Clemson answered right back with a touchdown. Hurts threw his only touchdown pass of the game to O. J. Howard to give Alabama a 10-point lead heading into the fourth quarter.

But the Tigers scored 14 points to take the lead with less than five minutes remaining in the game. Alabama had the ball, down by four, and needed a big drive from Hurts. The Tide were able to convert on a crucial fourth-and-one to keep the drive going, and a trick play got the ball down to the Clemson 30-yard line.

On the next play, Hurts took off down the sideline to score a touchdown. With just over two minutes left, the Tide were up by three, and it appeared that Hurts was about to win a national championship.

Watson was able to get the ball deep into Alabama territory, and with six seconds remaining, the Tide were called for pass interference. The ball was now on Alabama's two-yard line, with the game hanging in the balance. Rather than kick the field goal to tie the game, Clemson went for the win.

With one chance, Clemson ran a play that had some controversial results. Their inside receiver ran toward the cornerback, covering the outside receiver, and dove at his legs. The cornerback tripped up, leaving the outside receiver wide open. Watson hit him for the game-winning touchdown.

In most situations, the referee would have called offensive pass interference, but in this national championship, with the game on the line, the flag somehow stayed in his pocket, and Clemson got the win.

Just like that, Alabama's season was over. For Hurts, he was 13-1 as a true freshman. He ended the year with 2,780 passing yards and 23 touchdowns. He added 954 rushing yards and 13 touchdowns.

Sophomore Season

Every year at Alabama, dozens of football players leave for the NFL. They are quickly replaced by one of the best recruiting classes in the country. The 2017 offseason was no different. The Tide lost 10 starters, but they were about to be replaced by the number one recruiting class in the country.

For the Tide, their offense lost a number of weapons, but they returned Jalen Hurts, their starting quarterback. However, the Tide also brought in one of the best high school quarterbacks in the country to compete against Hurts. Tua Tagovailoa entered Alabama in the winter of 2017 to compete for the starting quarterback position. He was more of a true passing quarterback than Hurts. But Hurts had the advantage of having been in the system for a year.

But even Saban admitted that the Tide were limited in what they could do on the field with Hurts at quarterback.

"I think last year, the most difficult thing for a young quarterback to do is probably be a drop-back passer," Saban said. "So we try and create ways, and I'm being very positive, and I was in agreement with what we did, to try to create ways that we could throw the ball, make explosive plays in the passing game without doing a whole lot of drop-backs. Call it what you will, but it was because he was a freshman and we didn't want to ask him to do a lot of things that he wasn't comfortable doing. Is that a bad thing? We won 14 games that way. If we throw the ball a little bit better in the last game maybe it would have been different. But if we had played better defense the last three times they had the ball maybe that would have been different, too. I think we protected him a bit last year. It didn't enhance his development and sometimes later in the year when people played us in a way where we needed to be able to throw the ball, we may not have been efficient as we would have liked to have been. That's probably our fault as coaches."[xii]

Then came the Alabama spring game. Hurts barely played against the number-one defense in the country. Again, Saban and the coaching staff were protecting him. But while Hurts was watching from the sideline, Tagovailoa torched the second-team defense. He ended the game with 313 yards and 3 touchdowns. But despite that effort by the freshman, Hurts was still named the starter for week one against Florida State.

The Seminoles came into the game ranked third, while Alabama was the top-rated team in the nation despite losing the national championship to Clemson. The Tide were methodical and slowly took apart the Seminoles. They intercepted two passes and blocked two kicks.

Hurts only threw for 96 yards, 53 of which came on a touchdown to Calvin Ridley. But the Tide were able to take apart Florida State for a 24-7 win.

"It's good to get a win, but we have a lot of work to do," Alabama coach Nick Saban said before adding ominously for the rest of the nation: "We'll get better. It's one game. We have a long season. The focus that we have right now is what's ahead, not what's behind. This game tells us where we are, and where we need to go."[xiii]

Despite the slow start in the opening week win, the offense started clicking. Hurts rushed for more than 100 yards in back-to-back games for the first time in his career in out-of-conference wins over Fresno State and Colorado State. The Tide headed back to the SEC schedule with two easy games to start their conference slate.

Alabama blew out Vanderbilt and Ole Miss, scoring 125 points in two games. Hurts threw for three touchdowns and ran for another three touchdowns in those two games.

The Tide traveled to College Station to take on Texas A&M. Hurts ran for a touchdown and threw for one as Alabama was able to hold on for a 27-19 that was much closer than it should have been. The Aggies scored a late touchdown to get within one score, but Alabama was able to recover the onside kick to win the game.

Despite the win and being 6-0, Saban was still concerned that his players were listening to voices outside the program.

"I'm trying to get our players to listen to me instead of listening to you guys," he said, referring to reporters. "All that stuff that you write about how good we are and all that stuff they get on ESPN is like poison. It's like taking poison. Like rat poison. I'm asking them, 'Are you going to listen to me or are you going to listen to these guys about how good you are?'"[xiv]

Even Hurts started to see that the team was not where they wanted to be and that work needed to be done.

"Are we happy? Are we pleased? No," he said. "But we are happy that we can walk out of here with a win."[xv]

The Tide rebounded with blowout wins over Arkansas and Tennessee. Against the Razorbacks, Hurts threw his first interception of the season. But it was the *only* interception that he would throw all season.

Alabama hosted No. 19 LSU. The Tigers gave the Alabama offense fits in the previous season, holding them to just 10 points. This year was going to be different. Alabama took the opening drive down the field, using nine minutes of the clock. The drive ended with Hurts finding Irv Smith for a four-yard touchdown pass.

Hurts would add a third-quarter rushing touchdown, and the Alabama defense clamped down on the Tigers in a 24-10 win. Even Saban was pleased with the win.

"Jalen played a really good game," Saban said. "They played an eight-man front on us and made it really hard to run the ball. They ran people at the quarterback to try to take (Hurts) away from the running game. Some of the scrambles on third down were really key in the game, and he made some really good throws as well. When people play like that, you make some big plays, but it can get ugly in between, and that's how it was today, but I think he did a really good job out there. Obviously, this was a tough game. I told the players before the game that we had not had a hard test yet. Hard defines you in terms of who you are and we did not play a great game today. We had a lot of self-inflicted wounds but you can't be disappointed with the way our players fought, hung in there, and did what they had to do to win the game. You have to give LSU's players a lot of credit. This is always a tough and physical game, and it was certainly all of that tonight."[xv]

Alabama had a slight hangover the following week at No. 19 Mississippi State. The score was tied at 14 at the half, but the Bulldogs took a 24-17 lead early in the fourth quarter. Damien Harris tied the score at 24 with just over nine minutes left in the game.

As time was winding down, Alabama had the ball deep in Mississippi State territory. The offense was well within field goal range. Hurts came to the line with a run play called. He saw something in the defense and switched the play. He dropped back to pass and hit DeVonta Smith on a game-winning 26-yard touchdown pass.

"I saw something in the defense, so I told him to run the route I wanted him to run," Hurts said. "He kind of shook his head no at first, and I said, 'Trust me, I got you.'"[xvi]

The Tide escaped with a 31-24 win and kept the undefeated season intact for now.

"We did a good job of staying together, being one and staying cool and calm," Hurts said. "We did enough."[xvi]

After a blowout win over FCS Mercer, the Tide traveled to Auburn for the Iron Bowl. This time, it would pit the sixth-ranked Tigers against the top-ranked Tide. But for the first quarter and a half, the Alabama offense was non-existent.

On their first six third-down plays, the Tide did not convert a single first down. It took until the middle of the second quarter before Alabama converted on a third down play.

The Tigers took a 10-7 lead at the half, but Alabama took the second-half kickoff down the field for a go-ahead touchdown. But that would be the last touchdown they would score for the game.

Auburn would score the game's final 16 points to win 26-14. It would be Alabama's first loss of the season, and it knocked them out of the top ranking. It also put the College Football Playoff in jeopardy.

"We're going to learn from this," Hurts said. "It's humbling. The unfortunate thing about that (playoff) is it's not in our hands. You win out and you win games, you know you're in. We'll see what happens."[xvii]

Hurts only completed 12 passes in the game for 112 yards and a touchdown. This was the first game that started to show the Alabama coaches some of his limitations as a quarterback.

Alabama was able to sneak into the College Football Playoffs as the fourth seed. Their opening game would be against the Clemson Tigers. It would be the third year in a row that the two teams met in the CFP. In the previous two seasons, the teams met in the national championship game, with each team winning once.

Both offenses looked sluggish. The Tide did manage a touchdown pass in the first quarter. Clinging to a 10-6 lead, the Alabama defense scored two touchdowns in the third quarter to give Alabama a 24-6 win over defending champion Clemson. One of the touchdowns was a pass to defensive lineman Daron Payne after an interception set up the touchdown.

In two games against top-ranked opponents, Hurts and the Alabama offense struggled. Hurts threw for a total of 232 yards in two games. He only completed 28 passes.

After winning the Sugar Bowl, Alabama was now going to take on SEC Champion Georgia for the national championship. Both offenses struggled in the opening quarter, but Georgia was able to put up 13 points in the second quarter.

Alabama went into the half down 13-0. Hurts had only completed three passes for 21 yards in the half. At halftime, Saban decided to bench Hurts for the remainder of the game and go with the freshman Tagovailoa. In two seasons as the starter at Alabama, Hurts had only lost two games and won 26, but now he was going to be a spectator as someone else tried to lead his team to the national championship.

In the stands, as the two teams went into the locker room, Averion Hurts, Jalen's father and football coach, told his mother that Saban was going to bench Hurts. The elder Hurts knew that his son was struggling, and it was the right thing to do.

The decision did not look so great at first, however, as Tagovailoa threw an interception on Alabama's first drive of the half. But he rebounded and hit Henry Ruggs III on a six-yard touchdown pass to bring Alabama within six.

After a Georgia touchdown, Alabama managed two field goals to get within seven. With less than four minutes remaining in the game, Tagovailoa hit Calvin Ridley for the game-tying score. The game was headed to overtime.

The Bulldogs got the ball first, and after a huge sack, Georgia had to settle for a field goal. Then, on Alabama's first play, Tagovailoa took a 16-yard loss on a sack. Now, the Tide had the ball on the 41-yard line, completely out of field goal range.

Tagovailoa dropped back and found a wide-open Smith. He glided into the end zone as confetti started to reign down on the Tide. Alabama won the national championship on the game's final play.

"I could not believe it," Saban said. "There's lots of highs and lows. Last year we lost on the last play of the game and this year we won on the last play of the game. These kids really responded the right way. We said last year, `Don't waste the feeling.' They sure didn't, the way they played tonight."[xviii]

Hurts handled the situation about as well as anyone could. He was on the sideline helping Tagovailoa any way that he could and cheering his teammates on. When Alabama won the game, it was Hurts who was in the middle of the celebrating players.

"He just stepped in and did his thing," Hurts said. "He's built for stuff like this. I'm so happy for him."[xviii]

Tagovailoa was named the game's MVP after throwing three touchdowns and 166 yards in a half of football. There was going to be a quarterback controversy at Alabama the following season, but for now, the Tide were the National Champions.

"I just thought we had to throw the ball, and I felt he could do it better, and he did," Saban said of Tagovailoa and his decision to bench Hurts. "He did a good job, made some plays in the passing game. Just a great win. I'm so happy for Alabama fans. Great for our players. Unbelievable."[xviii]

After the game, Hurts went back to his hotel room with his family. The crowds and teammates were gone, and he was alone with the reality that he had been replaced on the biggest stage and his successor had won his team a national championship. Hurts started crying in his hotel room.

"He asked me, 'What are we going to do now?'" Averion Hurts said. "I told him, 'We don't have any choice. We've got to fight.' That quickly, it's like, OK, these people don't love you. They just love what you do when it makes them feel good."[xix]

In the moment, it was incredibly painful for Hurts, but it would be moments like this that would propel him to greatness in the NFL.

"It made me who I am," Hurts later reflected. "I think it put on a pedestal who I was as a person. I don't think it made me, technically, but I think it put on a pedestal the character that I was raised with. My father and my mother raised me to be a determined young man, a respectful young man, a man of character. I think in that moment, it was on display."[xix]

Shortly after the game, Hurts sought out Alabama offensive coordinator Mike Locksley, who would go on to become the head coach at Maryland. Hurts was considering transferring after losing out on the starting job in the national championship game, but Locksley tried to talk him out of it. But at the time, Hurts' pride was damaged.

"He didn't like it, but he respects it," Locksley said. "He said to me, 'I was 26-2 as a starter and now I'm not the starter anymore. What do I tell people? How do I explain this? How do I walk around campus?"[xix]

Nevertheless, Hurts made the decision to stay at Alabama and try to win back the starting quarterback position.

Junior Year

In the spring of 2018, the battle was on, but it was going to have to wait until the fall. In spring practice, Tagovailoa broke his left index finger. He was throwing a pass and hit his hand on a lineman's helmet. He would have to have surgery to repair the finger, but he would be ready for the fall.

This gave Jalen Hurts a chance to take over the job, but in the Alabama spring game, Hurts was outplayed by redshirt freshman Mac Jones. Jones came to Alabama the same year as Tagovailoa but was forced to redshirt his first year on campus. This meant that for the first time in the history of Alabama football, the team would have three future NFL starters on the roster. Jones is presently the starting quarterback of the New England Patriots.

Saban ordered both of his quarterbacks to remain silent, but once they returned to campus, the reporters swarmed both of them to get their feelings about the quarterback battle. To complicate matters, just before the 2018 season, the NCAA passed a rule that allowed players to transfer without having to sit out a season. The transfer portal, as it would become known, allowed players more freedom, especially if they weren't playing at one school, as they could now easily find another to take them.

Rumors started swirling about both Hurts and Tagovailoa transferring if they did not win the starting job, but they both refuted those rumors.

"The funniest thing about all of it is I've never said a thing," Hurts said. "I kept my mouth closed, didn't say anything to anyone. In regard to people believing the things that are said, it's hard to believe someone when the No. 1 source didn't say anything. There was never a decision needed to be made with regard to me leaving. That was something the general media placed on me. It was something I never said. It's just always been the elephant in the room, and it's like, for me, no one came up to me the whole spring, coaches included. No one asked me how I felt. No one asked me what was on my mind. No one asked me about how I felt about the things that were going on. Nobody asked me what my future held, and that's that. So now it's like, when we try and kind of handle the situation now, for me, it's kind of late. It's too late. The narrative has already been created."[xx]

As the season got closer, it appeared that Tagovailoa was going to win the starting job for the Tide. The rumors again started to spread that Hurts might transfer. Saban added fuel to that fire, when just before the season, he was asked if he thought that Hurts would be on the roster for Alabama's Week 1 game against Louisville.

"Well, I have no idea. I expect him to be there," Saban said. "I think it's our job to give both players a very fair opportunity to have a chance to win the team at their position. I think that one of the two guys—obviously, both are capable. We'll create a role for one or both of those guys on our team, and they'll all have to make a decision based on what that outcome is as to what their future is at Alabama."[xx]

Hurts's father added to the intrigue when he told reporters that his son would be the "biggest free agent" in college football if he decided to leave Alabama. But as the season approached, and with his only options to sit out the season or play as Alabama's backup, Hurts decided to stay with the Tide and watch Tagovailoa play quarterback.

Hurts played mostly in mop-up time in Alabama's first three wins. The Tide rolled over Louisville, Arkansas State, and Ole Miss, averaging 56 points a game. Hurts, despite his limited playing time, threw four touchdowns in those three games.

Alabama cruised through the regular season with Hurts playing in every game, but not getting time in any meaningful parts of the game. The closest game the Tide played was a 24-0 victory over Ole Miss. Every other game was a blowout, as the offense cruised with Tagovailoa at the helm.

The Tide took on the Georgia Bulldogs in the SEC Championship game. The Bulldogs defense put a beating on Tagovailoa throughout the game. When the offense would come off the field, he would head to the medical tent, but Tagovailoa came out every time to take the field. Hurts kept watching and waiting for his turn.

Early in the third quarter, the Bulldogs took a 14-point lead, and it appeared as though the Tide were going to lose their first game of the season. But with three minutes remaining in the quarter, Tagovailoa hit

Jaylen Waddle on a 51-yard touchdown pass to get Alabama within a touchdown.

With just over 11 minutes remaining in the game, Tagovailoa dropped back to pass, and one of his offense linemen stepped on his right ankle. The high ankle sprain ended his game. Hurts came onto the field to take over the team again.

With just over five minutes left, Hurts hit Jerry Jeudy on a 10-yard touchdown to tie the game. After a Georgia punt, Alabama got the ball back with a chance to win the game. With 3:02 left in the game, Hurts deftly moved the ball down the field.

With just over a minute left, Hurts took off running, broke a tackle, and scrambled into the end zone with the game-winning touchdown. After spending most of the season on the bench, Hurts rallied the Tide to win the SEC Championship.

"I've probably never been more proud of a player than Jalen," coach Nick Saban said. "It's unprecedented to have a guy that won as many games as he won ... start as a freshman, only lose a couple of games the whole time that he was the starter, and then all of a sudden he's not the quarterback. How do you manage that? How do you handle that? You've got to have a tremendous amount of class and character to put team first, knowing your situation is not what it used to be."[xxi]

Hurts ended the game with 82 yards passing, 28 yards rushing, and two touchdowns. He had also redeemed himself.

"It kind of feels like I'm breaking my silence," Hurts said. "I know at Alabama, there's always an opportunity to win. I'm so happy, so happy for everybody."[xxi]

But, despite the win and Hurts's exceptional play, he was back on the bench when Alabama played Oklahoma in the College Football Playoffs. The Tide would blow out the Sooners and once again take on Clemson for the College Football National

Championship. In the blowout loss to the Tigers, Hurts only got the opportunity to throw two passes. But with the end of the season, Hurts's career at Alabama was also ending.

It was precisely then that the NCAA announced that college athletes would no longer have to sit out the season if they decided to transfer.

"We had a conversation. [Hurts] wanted to graduate from Alabama, so he wasn't going to transfer until he graduated," Saban said. "I said, 'You need to work on becoming a better passer. You can't just make plays with your feet. So this whole season, I want you to focus in practice on reading coverages, understanding the passing game better, and being able to read and dissect what you need to do quickly'"... "And his diligence in doing that on a daily basis—he wouldn't take off in practice, he made himself stand in the pocket and learn how to do that. I said, 'You need to go to Oklahoma. They got the best coach to develop you as a quarterback. And you're going to be around the best players, so that's going to enhance your chances of having success.' He did that."[xxii]

Thus, Jalen Hurts took Nick Saban's advice. He was headed to Oklahoma to play for Lincoln Riley and the Sooners.

Oklahoma

Oklahoma Sooner's head coach, Lincoln Riley, had become somewhat of a quarterback guru. He was the first coach in NCAA football history to have back-to-back Heisman Trophy-winning quarterbacks. And now, he was able to get his hands on former Alabama star Jalen Hurts. It seemed like a match made in heaven. Hurts needed to work on his passing game, and Riley had just produced back-to-back, number-one overall draft picks in the NFL. The two needed each other in hopes of building another winning season.

In his first game with the Sooners, Hurts proved that he was still one of the best quarterbacks in college football. Against Houston, Hurts accounted for Oklahoma's first six touchdowns of the game. He threw for three and ran for another three in a blowout win over the Cougars.

"He played good," Riley said. "There were things he could do better, but I thought he handled the moment good. You could tell out there that he'd been in it, certainly. I'm sure he had some nerves, but he did a good job managing them."[xxiii]

But despite the win and the six touchdowns, Hurts still was not satisfied with his game.

"We did some really good things out there tonight, but there are a lot of things we can improve on," he said. "We've got to take that next step."[xxiii]

Hurts finished the game with 332 yards passing and another 176 yards rushing. He continued to dominate the next week against FCS South Dakota, and then against UCLA. He threw six more touchdowns, giving him nine through three games.

He added another five touchdowns in Big 12 wins over Texas Tech and Kansas, but the game that everyone cared about was next. Jalen Hurts had to prove himself with a win over archrival Texas.

Early in the third quarter, Texas kicked a field goal to tie the game at 10. It was the first time that Oklahoma did not lead in the game. But Hurts drove the Sooners right down the field and hit CeeDee Lamb on a 51-yard touchdown to take the lead for good.

Hurts and Lamb hooked up for their third touchdown in the game early in the fourth quarter to put the game out of reach. And just for good measure, Hurts ran a touchdown in with just over four minutes remaining. It would be a convincing win over No. 11 Texas. But even still, Hurts was not satisfied.

"I would say I didn't put the team in the greatest and best situation," said Hurts. "Not a complete game, but a step in the right direction."[xxiv]

Hurts ended his first and only Red River Rivalry with 235 yards passing and 3 touchdowns. He added 131 rushing yards and a touchdown. After six games, Hurts had 17 passing touchdowns and 8 rushing touchdowns.

After crushing West Virginia, the Sooners traveled to Kansas State. The Sooners jumped out to an early 10-0 lead thanks to a Hurts 10-yard rushing touchdown, but Skylar Thompson and the Wildcats would come right back. Both Hurts and Thompson rushed for two touchdowns in the first half, but the Wildcats were still up by a point at the half.

The third quarter was dominated by Kansas State. The much-maligned Sooner defense just could not stop Thompson. He rushed for two more touchdowns in the third quarter, and after an early fourth-quarter touchdown, the Wildcats were up 48-23.

Hurts and the Sooner offense mounted a feverish comeback in the fourth quarter, but even after another

Hurts touchdown run and a touchdown pass, the Sooners lost their first game of the season 48-41.

"We've got to be more appreciative, cherish every moment, and attack every moment with the right intent," Hurts said after the loss. For Hurts, it was his first loss as a starter in nearly two years. "We've got to learn from this and appreciate this lesson."[xxv]

The sting of that first loss would stay with Oklahoma's defense into the following week's game against Iowa State. Hurts threw for three touchdowns and ran for another two, giving Oklahoma what seemed like a comfortable 42-21 lead heading into the fourth quarter. But Iowa State scored 20 unanswered points in the quarter to get within one. Then, with less than 30 seconds remaining, Iowa State scored and went for the two-point conversion and the win. Luckily, Brock Purdy's pass was intercepted in the end zone, and Oklahoma narrowly escaped with a one-point victory.

Oklahoma seemed to be reeling as they headed to Baylor to take on the No. 11-ranked Bears. Baylor jumped all over Oklahoma in the first quarter and a half, building a daunting 28-3 lead.

After a Hurts touchdown pass, Baylor kicked a field goal to take a 31-10 lead into the half. But Jalen Hurts dominated the second half. He threw three touchdown passes to tie the game, and with less than four minutes remaining, he drove the Sooners down the field to kick the game-winning field goal.

"I put us in a horrible situation and we found a way to come back," Hurts said. "We overcame adversity, and you're remembered for what you do in November. So it's a big-time win today."[xxvi]

The conference schedule did not lighten up for the Sooners after the comeback against Baylor. Next up was TCU. Hurts rushed for two touchdowns and threw for two more as the Sooners held on for a 28-24 victory.

With a victory over rival Oklahoma State, the Sooners would clinch a spot in the Big 12 Championship Game. Strangely enough, Hurts ran for a touchdown, threw a touchdown, and even *caught* a touchdown pass in the blowout win over the Cowboys. That win set up a rematch against Baylor for the Big 12 title. A win would give Oklahoma a case for the College Football Playoff, but a loss would end those hopes.

After the first quarter, the Sooners took a 10-0 lead, and it looked like they were going to blow out the Bears. But Baylor owned the second quarter, putting up 13 points to take a 13-10 halftime lead.

But after a field goal, Hurts threw his only touchdown pass of the game to take a 20-13 lead. Then, after Oklahoma opened the fourth quarter with a field goal, Baylor scored 10 unanswered points to tie the score, and the game was headed to overtime.

Oklahoma got the ball first and scored on a five-yard touchdown run. After two incompletes, the Oklahoma defense got a sack to make it fourth and long. They were able to get an incomplete pass on the game's final play, and Oklahoma won the Big 12 Championship game in overtime.

"We didn't play our best, but we beat a damn good team here today, and we're the champs," Riley said. "They played like they have the majority of this year. There's some great defense being played at the University of Oklahoma right now. Man, I'm proud of those guys."[xxvii]

The Sooners would have to wait to find out if they were headed to the College Football Playoffs. But while they waited, Hurts was invited to New York City for the Heisman Trophy ceremony.

Despite his gaudy stats, Hurts finished second in the Heisman voting to Joe Burrow of LSU. Burrow had led the Tigers to the top seed in the College Football Playoff, an SEC Championship, and an undefeated regular season. He had also beaten Hurts's old team, Alabama.

"It was a very eventful weekend that only happens once in a lifetime, especially for a guy like me who's in his last year of ball," Hurts said after the ceremony. "It was something that felt really special, especially considering the opportunity I had to expose my family to certain things that I experience. Having my family around was great. Just coming here (to OU), I think my whole purpose was to have opportunities to accomplish things that we want to accomplish as a team," he continued. "I think it's a great opportunity for us as a team, to take advantage of this time, work really hard and prepare to play our best ball. I'm anxious to get back with our guys and get back to work."[xxviii]

The reward for Hurts and the Sooners was the fourth seed in the College Football Playoffs and a chance to take on top-seeded LSU and their new Heisman Trophy winner, Burrow.

The Tigers absolutely blitzed the Sooners. Burrow threw seven touchdowns in the game. Hurts did not throw a single touchdown but did rush for two scores. Oklahoma would lose the game 63-28.

"We needed to take advantage of every opportunity we had against a team like this," Hurts said after the game. "We failed to do that."[xxix]

Hurts ended his one season at Oklahoma with 3,851 yards passing and 32 touchdowns. He added 1,298 yards rushing and another 20 touchdowns. In total, Hurts accounted for 53 touchdowns for the Sooners.

"Our time together was short. It was fun. He made me a better coach because his approach was really unique. It was fun and challenging at the same time to coach. He probably said the same thing about his experience with us," Riley said of Hurts. "Maybe more than anything, we would get him to loosen up a little bit.

Got him to relax. Jalen is a pretty serious, at times stoic, guy…We allowed him to be able to relax, enjoy, and play the game maybe a little bit more free flowing. What the guy's done, though, is … I've had all these coaches and I'm just trying to take the best of each one and I think that's why he's playing the way he is."xxx

And now, after four seasons in college football and having only lost four games as a starter, Jalen Hurts was on his way to the NFL.

NFL Draft

Projecting out what Jalen Hurts would be in the NFL was difficult for scouts. Even after his monster season at Oklahoma, a school that had just produced the last two first-overall draft picks, scouts were still concerned about Hurts's accuracy when throwing the football.

"A great example that I think is a comparison that you'll probably remember is Jason Kidd as a shooter. Jason Kidd, most of his career, he's one of my favorite players growing up, this guy couldn't shoot a lick," former scout Matt Manocherian said of Hurts. "That was the one real thing in his game that wasn't there. All of a sudden, by the time he leaves the NBA, he's like the all-time leader in three-pointers made. Obviously, he learned how to shoot. That part of his game changed and now look at basketball, everybody's shooting threes like crazy. That's become something where lots of people have realized, seven-footers have realized, that they can learn that skill over time. Maybe passing is like that."[xxxi]

ESPN's draft guru Mel Kiper Jr. gave Hurts a fourth-round grade and said that he could only be used in gadget-type plays. But Hurts's coach saw something in him that they knew would make him a productive NFL quarterback.

"I told every NFL team that came through the positives and negatives. The question from every team was how do you project this guy? And I told them all I think he's gonna be a really good player, he's got a pro mentality. But I said I don't know where his ceiling is because, at that point, he had five straight years of new offensive coordinators," said Riley. "I told somebody if he ever got some continuity in a system, watch out."[xxxii]

Hurts's former coach even thought that he would be a great player in the NFL.

"There's a lot of guys playing in the NFL now that are having a lot of success that are similar style players to Jalen, guys that can make plays with their feet. I think you know who they are," Alabama coach Nick Saban said of Hurts. "I think the success of those players has kind of broken the stereotype of, you got to be a drop-back passer and this is the only way you can win in the NFL. You see Mahomes, the guy in Baltimore, all these guys are athletic guys who make plays with their feet."[xxxiii]

Hurts performed well at the combine but was still considered the fourth- or fifth-best quarterback in the draft. This draft night would be unusual. With the COVID-19 pandemic then raging, the players would have to stay home and only be shown on a Zoom call.

The first pick in the 2020 NFL Draft was Heisman Trophy winner Joe Burrow. The next quarterback would be Tua Tagovailoa, who had ultimately beaten Hurts out at quarterback when the two were at Alabama. Right after Tagovailoa, Justin Herbert, out of Oregon, was selected by San Diego.

Jordan Love was selected by Green Bay at 26, and that would be the final quarterback selection in the first round. As the second round started to unfold, Hurts kept slipping down the draft. Finally, with the 53rd pick of the draft, the Philadelphia Eagles selected quarterback Jalen Hurts out of Oklahoma.

So, the Texas kid would be taking his talents to the City of Brotherly Love.

Chapter 3: Pro Career

Rookie Season

When Jalen Hurts arrived in Philadelphia, the team already had a starting quarterback. The Eagles had selected Carson Wentz out of North Dakota State with their first-round pick in 2016. Wentz was on his way to an MVP season when he blew out his knee. Nick Foles would take over at quarterback and lead the Eagles to their only Super Bowl victory in 2018.

It was still unclear exactly how the Eagles were going to use Jalen Hurts, but Philadelphia head coach Doug Pederson knew what he was looking for when the team drafted him.

"You go into drafts and you go into each year looking for quarterbacks," Pederson said. "And we continued to look for quarterbacks. That's always something that will never change. We won a Super Bowl with our backup quarterback, and we've had to play with our backup a couple of times in Philadelphia. And so we did that a year ago and brought in Jalen Hurts, not to undermine Carson Wentz, not to do anything to take his job or anything because Carson was definitely our starter. He was the franchise and all that moving forward. But someone that could come in and be the backup and learn how to play the NFL game. Bring his talent to the Philadelphia Eagles. And really just as the season began things just kind of, I guess, spiraled out of control. Injuries began to set in, we weren't playing very well, turnovers offensively, just a number of things, penalties, more injuries compounded problems. It just became harder and harder as the year wore on. No one or no one person is to blame for any of what happened last year."[xxxiv]

Despite Pederson's confidence in his rookie, Hurts did not play in either of Philadelphia's first two games, both of which were losses. He only played sparingly in the team's first 11 games. He would only come in for a play or two to run the ball, or as a gadget play.

But heading into the team's Week 13 game against Green Bay, the season was over. The Eagles were 3-7-1. Wentz had been disappointing throughout the season, and led the NFL in interceptions, fumbles, and number of times sacked. And he was struggling against Green Bay as well. The Eagles fell behind the Packers 23-3 in the fourth quarter, and Pederson decided to sit Wentz and let Hurts finish the game.

With Hurts leading the team, Philadelphia scored 14 points in just under two minutes to get back into the game. Hurts threw his first career touchdown pass. The defense allowed Green Bay to score a final touchdown to put the game out of reach, but Hurts showed what he could do under center.

After the game, Pederson made the decision to start Hurts the following week against New Orleans. The beleaguered Philly offense showed renewed vigor with the rookie at quarterback. At the end of the first quarter, the Eagles were up 17-0.

Philly would go on to win the game 24-21. The victory broke a four-game losing streak. Hurts ended his first start with 167 yards passing and 106 rushing yards. Two days after the victory, Pederson decided to start Jalen Hurts for the remainder of the season.

"After going through the film and really looking back even to last week and the preparation and everything, I'm gonna continue with Jalen this week as the starter," Pederson said. "You know, I was thinking of a lot of things. Quite honestly, I was thinking of Carson, but I was thinking about the rest of the team and how the rest of the team played in the game. Jalen did, after looking at the film again today, Jalen played well. He was a big part of the success we had on offense and obviously helping us win that football game, but there were a lot of other great individual performances on both sides of the ball. I think of Miles Sanders, I think of Josh Sweat, Javon Hargrave. Fletcher Cox had a big game, big sack. We had two defensive takeaways in the game. So there were a lot of positives coming out of the football game and I didn't want to say it was all about one guy. You guys know me and my answers. I've always been about the team and really that was a team win yesterday."[xxxv]

The next week, Philly traveled to the desert to take on the Arizona Cardinals and Hurts's fellow Oklahoma alum, Kyler Murray. Murray was the quarterback for the Sooners the season before Hurts had arrived on campus. Murray also won the Heisman Trophy and was the first overall pick in the draft.

The Cardinals jumped all over the Eagles in the first quarter, putting up 16 points. Hurts fought back in the second quarter, throwing three touchdowns. But Murray and the Cardinals still had a six-point lead at the half.

In the third quarter, Hurts had his first career rushing touchdown to tie the game. Late in the fourth quarter, Murray threw the game-winning touchdown pass. But Hurts had his best game as a pro. He threw for 338 yards and 3 touchdowns. He also ran for 63 yards and a touchdown.

"I hate to lose more than I love to win," Hurts said after the game. "It's not a great feeling but it's a learning lesson."[xxxvi]

Hurts and the Eagles would drop their final two games of the season to Dallas and Washington. Hurts had a solid final four games, but the team was only 1-3 in his four starts.

A week after the season ended, the Eagles fired head coach Doug Pederson. It was a controversial move, considering that Pederson had led the team to its only Super Bowl victory.

"My first allegiance is, what will be best for the Philadelphia Eagles and our fans for the next three, four, five years. It's not based on does someone deserve to hold their job or deserve to get fired; that's a different bar," team owner Jeffrey Lurie said. "It's not about, 'Did Doug deserve to be let go?' No, he did not deserve to be let go. That's not where I'm coming from, and that's not the bar in the evaluation process."[xxxvii]

But during the press conference, Lurie got confrontational with reporters after some suggested that Pederson was forced to continue playing Wentz over Hurts despite terrible results.

"I don't think any owner should decide that. Carson, to me and to I think virtually everyone in our organization, is a quarterback that in his first four years was in many ways elite, comparable to some of the great quarterbacks the first four years in the league. The fifth year, obviously not satisfactory for whatever reasons, there are probably multiple reasons for that," Lurie said. "I think the way I look at it is, we have an asset and we have a talent. He's a great guy. He wants nothing but to win big and win Lombardi trophies for Philadelphia. This guy is tireless. He has his heart in the right place. He is really dedicated offseason, on-season. He's just what you want. And it behooves us as a team with a new coach and new coaching staff to be able to really get him back to that elite progression where he was capable of, and understand at the same time that there have been many quarterbacks in their fourth and fifth year, if you trace this, you can come up with many, many quarterbacks that have a single year where it's just, 'Whoa, the touchdown-to-interception ratio is not what you want.' And we're talking some great ones like Peyton and Ben and guys like that. So I take more of a longer view of this was not the best season for our offense," Lurie continued. "It was a poor season. And we also had a poor season from Carson, in terms of what he's been able to show in the past; very fixable, and I fully expect him to realize his potential."[xxxvii]

But, shortly after Pederson's firing, Wentz asked to be traded. In March, the Eagles sent him to the Colts for a third-round draft pick. Jalen Hurts was now the starter for Philadelphia.

Second Season

To replace Pederson, the Eagles hired 39-year-old Nick Sirianni. Sirianni had been the offensive coordinator for the Indianapolis Colts, and he brought a new system and energy to an Eagles team that desperately needed it.

The starting quarterback job now belonged to Jalen Hurts. He showed that the Eagles had made the right decision in the opening game against the Falcons. Hurts threw three touchdown passes in the team's blowout win.

But the strong start didn't last. Philadelphia would drop six of their next eight games, putting them at 3-9 more than halfway through the season. But Hurts and the Eagles would win six of their next seven games to clinch a playoff spot. Philadelphia's only loss during that stretch came against the New York Giants. Hurts threw three interceptions but left the game with a high ankle sprain. He would miss one game, a victory over the Jets.

Philadelphia finished the year at 9-8 and tied for the final wild-card playoff spot with the New Orleans Saints. In Week 11, the Eagles beat the Saints, which gave them the tiebreaker over New Orleans. The Saints went home, and the Eagles went to the playoffs.

In his first playoff game, Hurts would be taking on a legend. Tom Brady and the Buccaneers were waiting for them. This would be Hurts's first playoff game. For Brady, it was just another day at the office.

Hurts threw two interceptions in the first half as the Bucs built a 17-0 halftime lead. In the third quarter, Brady threw his only two touchdown passes of the game to give Tampa Bay a 31-0 lead. The Eagles fought back in the fourth quarter, with Hurts throwing his first career playoff touchdown, but it was too little too late. The Eagles fell 31-15.

"We didn't play good enough today, I didn't play good enough today," said Hurts, who was wearing a protective boot on his left foot after the game. This game does not define us, does not define who we are. We know all the different things that we've overcome. I know as a football team we'll be back. We'll be back. This is a feeling that will kind of simmer in our hearts, simmer for us all."[xxxviii]

At 23, Hurts was the youngest quarterback to ever start a playoff game for the Eagles, but it wasn't enough for him. He had a solid second season, but he still wanted more. And more was about to come his way.

Super Bowl Season

Heading into the 2022 season, the Eagles were stacked with fresh talent. After being eliminated from the playoffs, the team brought in more than a dozen new players, mostly on one-year contracts. They were preparing for a big run, and that was exactly what happened.

The Eagles started the season by going 8-0 for the first time in franchise history. And it was not just that they were undefeated—they were blowing most teams out! The offense was clicking under Jalen's capable leadership, and the defense was shutting teams down. By all accounts, Nick Sirianni's sophomore season as a head coach was truly a transformational one for the team.

But the hope for an undefeated season came to an abrupt end in Week 10 against the Washington Commanders of all teams. The Commanders were struggling, but the Eagles played a sloppy game against an overmatched opponent. Ultimately, Washington was able to put together long drives that kept Philly's offense off the field. Even worse, most of those drives were helped along by numerous penalties committed by the Eagles defense. When the final bell sounded, Philadelphia lost its first game 32-21.

"It's the same message that's always been delivered after our wins, same message delivered after our losses, we're controlling the things we can," Hurts said. "We came here today, we didn't do that. And today it got us. It's very important to control the things that you can. Controlling your ball security."[xxxix]

After the sloppy loss, the Eagles quickly rebounded and were able to run off five straight wins. In their fifth win against Chicago, the season nearly ended for Hurts. Late in the third quarter, Hurts was scrambling and took a hit. He stayed down on the turf for a second and then went back to the huddle.

He was able to stay in the game for the final play of the third quarter, but in between quarters, he ran to the sideline to talk with the trainers. He told them that he thought he had broken his collarbone. The Eagles were only up 14-13 at the time, so Hurts stayed in the game and played through the pain.

Hurts was able to lead the Eagles down the field in the fourth quarter for a touchdown that would ice the game. Despite the cold, whipping wind and the pain in his throwing arm, he continued to play.

"It was so cold," he said. "I felt serious pain. I felt pain that I've never felt. I couldn't throw. I was having to throw the ball, too. It was so cold; the ball just wouldn't come out. Yeah, it wasn't easy. Being able to overcome everything that went on in that game, it took a lot. I'm happy I was able to find it in me."[xl]

After the game, Hurts was diagnosed with a sprained A/C joint in his right shoulder. The injury renders the shoulder unstable, which means that any movement will send pain shooting through the body. Hurts was able to play the entire fourth quarter in pain.

At that point in the season, the Eagles were 13-1 and had already clinched the NFC East title. They would only need one more win to clinch home-field advantage throughout the playoffs. But they were going to be without their quarterback for a few weeks.

Hurts sat out the next two weeks, losses to the Cowboys and Saints. He was able to return for the regular season finale against the Giants. He was steady but not spectacular in a 22-16 win.

The Eagles finished the season at 14-3. They set a franchise record for most wins in a season. Hurts ended the regular season with 3,701 passing yards and 22 touchdowns. He also rushed for 760 yards and 13 touchdowns. His 13 rushing touchdowns would be tied for the most in league history by a quarterback.

Hurts was named to his first Pro Bowl and was second team All-Pro. He also finished second in the MVP voting and third in the AP Offensive Player of the Year voting. He had arrived as a franchise quarterback, but now it was time to win a playoff game.

The Eagles opened up the divisional round of the playoffs against the New York Giants. With the week off, Hurts had more time to heal from his shoulder injury, and it showed. Philadelphia bombed the Giants. Hurts threw two touchdowns in the first quarter and ran for one in the second quarter as the Eagles took a 28-0 halftime lead. Philadelphia then continued to pour it on in the second half as they routed the visiting Giants 38-7.

"To have him out there, I know this is high praise, it's like having Michael Jordan out there," coach Nick Sirianni said of Hurts. "He's your leader. He's your guy. That's the biggest respect I can pay to him. This guy leads, he brings this calmness to the entire team. He's as tough as they come. To me, there's not anybody that's played better football than him this year."[xli]

The Eagles would host the San Francisco 49ers in the NFC Championship game. The 49ers were playing with their third-string quarterback, Brock Purdy, who had lost to Hurts when he was at Iowa State.

With the score tied at seven, the Eagles methodically took apart the 49ers. Purdy would hurt his shoulder in the game, and the 49ers would have to bring in their fourth-string quarterback. But the Eagles had already started to dominate the game. Philly would go on to win the game 31-7 and head back to the Super Bowl.

"I think as a football team, we came out and played with a lot of energy," Hurts said after the game. "We prepared well throughout the week, and we were always talking about challenging everybody to play their best ball. Because I truly never put a limit on myself, and I never put a limit on what this team can do. So there is always more out there for us to get. To come out there and play the way we did tonight—I'm proud of this group, I'm proud of this team, I'm proud of the preparation that we put in to get to where we are. A lot to be grateful for, but it was earned during the week. Excited to have another opportunity to play for something big again."[xlii]

The Eagles would be taking on the Kansas City Chiefs in the Super Bowl. The Chiefs had one of the best quarterbacks in the NFL in Patrick Mahomes. It would be a battle of two of the best players in the league, but it would also be a historic battle. For the first time in Super Bowl history, each team would start an African-American quarterback.

Hurts opened the scoring with a one-yard touchdown run, but Mahomes answered right back with a touchdown pass. Hurts and the Eagles would score the first half's final 10 points to take a 24-14 lead into the locker room.

But the Mahomes magic wasn't done. Down by six heading into the fourth quarter, the Chiefs scored two straight touchdowns to take a seven-point lead. Still, Hurts answered right back with his third rushing touchdown of the game to tie the score. But Mahomes was able to drive the Chiefs down the field to kick the game-winning field goal with five seconds left in the game. Just like that, the Chiefs were Super Bowl champions, and the Eagles weren't.

"You either win or you learn," Hurts said after the loss. "As always, win, lose, or draw, I always reflect on the things that I could've done better, the things we could've done better to try and take that next step. That'll be the same process that goes on now. You want to cherish these moments with the people that you've come so far with. You know, your family, loved ones, teammates, peers, everyone that you do it with and do it for. I will say I'm so proud of this team for everything that we've been able to overcome. Obviously, we had a big-time goal in the end that we wanted to accomplish, and we came up short. I think the beautiful part about it is everyone experiences different pains, different agonies of life but you decide if you want to learn from it, you decide if you want to use that to be a teachable moment and I know what I'll do."[xliii]

Despite the loss, Jalen Hurts had one of the best Super Bowls in NFL history. He tied a Super Bowl record with three rushing touchdowns. He also threw for 304 yards and a touchdown. But even that was not enough, as the Eagles ultimately lost the game.

After the season ended, Hurts signed a record-setting contract with the Eagles. The extension was for $255 million until 2028. It would make Hurts the highest-paid quarterback in the NFL with $51 million per season, passing Mahomes.

"I'm not telling you anything you don't know here, but seeing him virtually every day, he's got an incredible passion for being phenomenal," team owner Jeffrey Lurie said. "You see that in the great ones. We all know in other sports and with certain quarterbacks in this league, you can define them by their obsession with detail and work ethic."[xliv]

And just like that, Jalen Hurts has established himself as one of the best quarterbacks in the NFL, and he will no doubt be dominating the NFL for years to come. At the time of this writing, late into the 2023-24 season, Hurts has been simply incredible, and the Eagles are flying high once again. They sit at the top of the NFL with a 10-1 record, the best in the entire league, and seem poised to storm right back to the Super Bowl once more.

Chapter 4: Personal Life

Jalen Hurts is not currently married; however, he does have a long-term relationship. He and Bryonna Burrows met in 2016 while they were both students at Alabama. Burrows graduated from Alabama with a degree in political science and went back to Tuscaloosa to get her MBA.

After her graduation, Bry took a job with IBM in Dallas, Texas. The distance between the two made the relationship difficult for a while, but the couple made their public debut after the NFC Championship game in 2023. It was the first time that they were seen together in public, despite dating on and off for nearly seven years.

Like nearly everything that Hurts does, he keeps his private life very private. Neither Hurts nor Burrows puts their relationship on social media. The only way that the public knew they were dating was when she joined Hurts on the field after the Eagles won the NFC Championship.

Besides his mother and Burrows, Hurts has a third woman in his life. His agent, Nicole Lynn, is the first African-American female to represent a starting quarterback in the NFL.

"Her being an African American female, so many different things you gotta overcome. Doing that in any field, let alone a male-dominated field, and being an agent in football and in sports," Hurts said. "It's tough, but it's nothing she can't handle. That's why we are [working] together, because we both have that mentality. We both have that approach to everything we do."[xlv]

Hurts has also made charity work a large part of his young career. During COVID, he worked with Alex's Lemonade Stand to donate $30,000 to a young man battling cancer in Philadelphia. He also personally donated $10,000 to the Latin Charter School.

Being from Texas, Hurts knows food. He recently worked with Louisiana Hot Sauce to create the Jalen Hurts Signature Hot Sauce. It is only available online, and Hurts has decided that all of the proceeds will go to the OneMindSet Foundation.

The Foundation was founded by his former Oklahoma teammate, Chanse Sylvie. The organization offers a range of mentorship, tutoring, sports training, and seminar programs to teach young people varying life lessons, from financial literacy to job preparation to overcoming the barriers of systemic racism.

For the past two years, just before Christmas, Hurts has participated in the "Day of Care." It's an eight-hour tour of schools throughout the Philadelphia area. Hurts spends the day meeting with students and giving out gift cards and presents.

"I think when you have mentorship, you have mentors around you, you have people that are trying to help you dream on it, that's something that's a resource that you have to use," Hurts said. "So if you can get the kids to understand that early, get the kids to understand what true trust and friendship looks like–because everybody is not your friend."[xlvi]

If there is anyone who knows how to overcome adversity, it is Jalen Hurts. He overcame a demoralizing public benching to become one of the best quarterbacks in the NFL. And now the future is his.

Chapter 5: Legacy

Jalen Hurts's NFL legacy is still being written. He has only been a starter in the league for two full seasons. But in those two seasons, he has proven that he is one of the best quarterbacks in the NFL. He was able to lead the Philadelphia Eagles to the Super Bowl for only the fifth time in team history, and appears to be in the process of doing it once again in his third season.

Hurts also tied the Super Bowl record with three rushing touchdowns. He was nearly the second player in Super Bowl history to win the MVP award while on a losing team. (Chuck Howley was the only other player to win the MVP on a losing team in Super Bowl V for the Dallas Cowboys.) And if it were not for an injury late in the season, Hurts would have been the league's MVP over Patrick Mahomes.

Hurts is now in the perfect position to build on his legacy. The Philadelphia Eagles are a young team with a number of great players to put around Hurts, not to mention an emerging star in their young head coach, Nick Sirianni. Indeed, they have resumed their winning ways in the 2023-24 NFL season, now at 10-1. Not only did Hurts and his Eagles take down the Buffalo Bills in Week 10 (helmed by none other than Tua Tagovailoa!), but they also triumphed over Mahomes and the Kansas City Chiefs in a *Monday Night Football* matchup that was billed as a Super Bowl rematch. To say Hurts's future as an Eagle looks promising is putting it mildly!

And, despite all the quarterback controversy at Alabama and his ultimate transfer to Oklahoma, you cannot look back at Hurts's college career as anything but a great success. As a college player, Hurts is undoubtedly a future College Football Hall-of-Famer. In three years as a starter, he only lost four games. He is also one of only a handful of college football players with more than 3,000 passing yards and 1,000 rushing yards in a season. He also won a national championship and SEC championships while at

Alabama and a Big 12 Championship while at Oklahoma, making him one of the only quarterbacks to win league championships in two different leagues.

Hurts has established himself as one of the best quarterbacks in the NFL after overcoming some very public adversity. Very few people would have come back from that, but that's the kind of person Jalen Hurts is. Now a beloved and respected leader in Philadelphia with a long career ahead of him, the football—and his destiny—are in his hands, and we cannot wait to see how his future unfolds.

Final Word/About the Author

I was born and raised in Norwalk, Connecticut. Growing up, I could often be found spending many nights watching basketball, soccer, and football matches with my father in the family living room. I love sports and everything that sports can embody. I believe that sports are one of the most genuine forms of competition, heart, and determination. I write my works to learn more about influential athletes in the hopes that from my writing, you the reader can walk away inspired to put in an equal if not greater amount of hard work and perseverance to pursue your goals. If you enjoyed *Jalen Hurts: The Inspiring Story of One of Football's Star Quarterbacks,* please leave a review! Also, you can read more of my works on *David Ortiz, Cody Bellinger, Alex Bregman, Francisco Lindor, Shohei Ohtani, Ronald Acuna Jr., Javier Baez, Jose Altuve, Christian Yelich, Max Scherzer, Mookie Betts, Pete Alonso, Clayton Kershaw, Mike Trout, Bryce Harper, Jackie Robinson, Justin Verlander, Derek*

Jeter, Ichiro Suzuki, Ken Griffey Jr., Babe Ruth, Aaron Judge, Novak Djokovic, Roger Federer, Rafael Nadal, Serena Williams, Naomi Osaka, Coco Gauff, Baker Mayfield, George Kittle, Matt Ryan, Matthew Stafford, Eli Manning, Khalil Mack, Davante Adams, Terry Bradshaw, Jimmy Garoppolo, Philip Rivers, Von Miller, Aaron Donald, Joey Bosa, Josh Allen, Mike Evans, Joe Burrow, Carson Wentz Adam Thielen, Stefon Diggs, Lamar Jackson, Dak Prescott, Patrick Mahomes, Odell Beckham Jr., J.J. Watt, Colin Kaepernick, Aaron Rodgers, Tom Brady, Russell Wilson, Peyton Manning, Drew Brees, Calvin Johnson, Brett Favre, Rob Gronkowski, Andrew Luck, Richard Sherman, Bill Belichick, Candace Parker, Skylar Diggins-Smith, A'ja Wilson, Lisa Leslie, Sue Bird, Diana Taurasi, Julius Erving, Clyde Drexler, John Havlicek, Oscar Robertson, Ja Morant, Gary Payton, Khris Middleton, Michael Porter Jr., Julius Randle, Jrue Holiday, Domantas Sabonis, Mike Conley Jr., Jerry West, Dikembe Mutombo, Fred

VanVleet, Jamal Murray, Zion Williamson, Brandon Ingram, Jaylen Brown, Charles Barkley, Trae Young, Andre Drummond, JJ Redick, DeMarcus Cousins, Wilt Chamberlain, Bradley Beal, Rudy Gobert, Aaron Gordon, Kristaps Porzingis, Nikola Vucevic, Andre Iguodala, Devin Booker, John Stockton, Jeremy Lin, Chris Paul, Pascal Siakam, Jayson Tatum, Gordon Hayward, Nikola Jokic, Bill Russell, Victor Oladipo, Luka Doncic, Ben Simmons, Shaquille O'Neal, Joel Embiid, Donovan Mitchell, Damian Lillard, Giannis Antetokounmpo, Chris Bosh, Kemba Walker, Isaiah Thomas, DeMar DeRozan, Amar'e Stoudemire, Al Horford, Yao Ming, Marc Gasol, Draymond Green, Kawhi Leonard, Dwyane Wade, Ray Allen, Pau Gasol, Dirk Nowitzki, Jimmy Butler, Paul Pierce, Manu Ginobili, Pete Maravich, Larry Bird, Kyle Lowry, Jason Kidd, David Robinson, LaMarcus Aldridge, Derrick Rose, Paul George, Kevin Garnett, Michael Jordan, LeBron James, Kyrie Irving, Klay Thompson, Stephen Curry, Kevin Durant, Russell Westbrook,

Chris Paul, Blake Griffin, Kobe Bryant, Anthony Davis, Joakim Noah, Scottie Pippen, Carmelo Anthony, Kevin Love, Grant Hill, Tracy McGrady, Vince Carter, Patrick Ewing, Karl Malone, Tony Parker, Allen Iverson, Hakeem Olajuwon, Reggie Miller, Michael Carter-Williams, James Harden, John Wall, Tim Duncan, Steve Nash, Gregg Popovich, Pat Riley, John Wooden, Steve Kerr, Brad Stevens, Red Auerbach, Doc Rivers, Erik Spoelstra, Mike D'Antoni, and *Phil Jackson* in the Kindle Store. If you love football, check out my website at claytongeoffreys.com to join my exclusive list where I let you know about my latest books and give you lots of goodies.

Like what you read? Please leave a review!

I write because I love sharing the stories of influential athletes like Jalen Hurts with fantastic readers like you. My readers inspire me to write more so please do not hesitate to let me know what you thought by leaving a review! If you love books on life, sports, or productivity, check out my website at claytongeoffreys.com to join my exclusive list where I let you know about my latest books. Aside from being the first to hear about my latest releases, you can also download a free copy of *33 Life Lessons: Success Principles, Career Advice & Habits of Successful People.* See you there!

Clayton

References

[i] Caruso, Skyler. "All About Jalen Hurts' Parents, Averion and Pamela Hurts." People Magazine. Feb. 9, 2023.

[ii] March, Lochlahn. "Jalen Hurts Had A Bryce Harper Poster on His Wall Growing Up." The Philadelphia Inquirer. Aug. 21, 2023.

[iii] Berman, Zach. "Eagles' Jalen Hurts Returns To Houston for First NFL Game in His Hometown" The Athletic. Nov. 1, 2022.

[iv] Justice, Richard. "Texas Football Coaches Recall Jalen Hurts' Dominance." Texas Monthly. Feb. 9, 2023.

[v] Zenitz, Matt. "Meet Alabama's Promising Freshman Quarterback and Former Powerlifter." AL.Com. July 20, 2016. Web.

[vi] Champlin, Drew. "Texas Dual-Threat QB Jalen Hurts Commits to Alabama." AL.Com. June 6, 2015. Web.

[vii] Sabin, Rainer. "Alabama's Top Moments of 2016." AL.Com. Dec. 29, 2016. Web.

[viii] "Hurts, Alabama Defense Led the Way to 49-30 Win over Arkansas." ESPN.Com Oct. 8, 2016. Web.

[ix] "No. 1 Alabama Trounces No 9 Tennessee in 49-10 runaway." ESPN.Com. Oct. 15, 2016 Web.

[x] "No. 1 Alabama Extends Winning Streak Against No. 13 LSU, 10-0." ESPN.Com. Nov. 6, 2016. Web.

[xi] "Football Vs. Florida Postgame Quotes." Roll Tide.Com. Dec. 3, 2016. Web.

[xii] Sabin, Rainer. "Nick Saban 'In Agreement' With Plan to Protect Alabama QB Jalen Hurts." AL.Com. April 21, 2017. Web.

[xiii] "No. 1 Alabama Defense Smothers No 3 Florida State 24-7." ESPN.Com. Sept. 3, 2017. Web.

[xiv] "Harris Helps No. 1 Alabama Outlast Texas A&M 27-19." ESPN.Com. Oct. 8, 2017 Web.

[xv] "Football Vs LSU Postgame Quotes." Roll Tide.Com. Nov. 4, 2017. Web.

[xvi] "Late TD Lifts Alabama Over Mississippi State." ESPN.Com. Nov. 11, 2017. Web.

[xvii] "No 6 Auburn Tops No. 1 Alabama 26-14, Earns SEC Title Shot." ESPN.Com. Nov. 25, 2017. Web.

[xviii] "Walk Off: Alabama Beats Georgia in OT For National Title." ESPN.Com. Jan. 8, 2018 Web.

[xix] Longman, Jere. "Born for the Storm: How Jalen Hurts Learned to be Unflappable." The New York Times. Dec. 20, 2022.

[xx] Staples, Andy. "Jalen Hurts Has Broken His Silence And Alabama's

Quarterback Battle is On." Sports Illustrated. Aug. 6, 2018.

[xxi] "Hurts Rallies No. 1 Alabama to 35-28 Win Over No. 4 Georgia." ESPN.Com Dec. 2, 2018. Web.

[xxii] Andres, Patrick. "Nick Saban Details Advice He Gave Jalen Hurts Before QB's Transfer to Oklahoma." Sports Illustrated. Feb. 5, 2023.

[xxiii] "Hurts Has 6 TDs, No 4 Oklahoma Beats Houston 49-31." ESPN.Com. Sept. 2, 2019. Web.

[xxiv] "Lamb TDs, Defense Lifts No 6 Oklahoma Past No. 11 Texas." ESPN.Com. Oct. 12, 2019. Web.

[xxv] "Skyler Thompson, K-State Stun No 5 Oklahoma 48-41." ESPN.Com. Oct. 27, 2019. Web.

[xxvi] "Sooners Fight Back to Beat Baylor." Sooner Wire.Com. Nov. 16, 2019. Web.

[xxvii] "Sooners Win Big 12 Title in Overtime Thriller." Sooners Wire.Com. Dec. 7, 2019. Web.

[xxviii] "Hurts Finishes Runner-Up for the Heisman." Sooners Sports.Com. Dec. 14, 2019. Web.

[xxix] "Burrow Throws 7 TDs, No. 1 LSU Routs No 4 Oklahoma 63-28." ESPN.Com. Dec. 28, 2019. Web.

[xxx] Gillenwater, Sam. "Lincoln Riley Recalls his Time Coaching Jalen Hurts." On3.Com. Oct. 12, 2022. Web.

[xxxi] McMullen, John. "Former NFL Scout on Jalen Hurts: Maybe We Can Teach Him Accuracy." Sports Illustrated. March 31, 2022.

[xxxii] Gillenwater, Sam. "Lincoln Riley Recalls his Time Coaching Jalen Hurts." On3.Com. Oct. 12, 2022. Web.

[xxxiii] "Mel Kiper Jr. Shares his Draft Grade for Jalen Hurts." Saturday Down South.Com. March 6, 2020. Web.

[xxxiv] Inabinett, Mark. "Doug Pederson Still Answering Questions About Jalen Hurts." AL.Com. July 11, 2021. Web.

[xxxv] Patra, Kevin. "Doug Pederson Confirms Jalen Hurts Will Remain Eagles Starting QB in Week 15." NFL.Com. Dec. 14, 2020. Web.

[xxxvi] "Murray, Hopkins Lead Cardinals Past Eagles, 33-26." ESPN.Com. December 20, 2020. Web.

[xxxvii] McManus, Tim. "Philadelphia Eagles Change Course, Fire Head Coach Doug Pederson After Five Seasons." ESPN.Com. Jan. 11, 2021. Web.

[xxxviii] "Brady Throws 2 TDs, Super Bowl Champions Dominate Eagles 31-15." ESPN.Com. Jan. 16, 2022. Web.

[xxxix] "Commanders End Sloppy Eagles Perfect Season 32-21." ESPN.Com. Nov. 15, 2022. Web.

[xl] Bishop, Greg. "Jalen Hurts and the Shoulder He Survived." Sports